My Dad, My Hero

Thoughts on Fatherhood

My Dad, My Hero

Thoughts on Fatherhood

Edited by Heather Russell-Revesz

BARNES
&NOBLE
BOOKS
NEW YORK

For my Dad.

The quotes in this book have been drawn from many sources, and are assumed to be accurate as quoted in their previously published forms. Although every effort has been made to verify the quotes and sources, the publisher cannot guarantee their perfect accuracy.

2003 Barnes & Noble Books

ISBN 0-7607-4061-5

Printed and bound in the United States of America

M 9 8 7 6 5 4 3 2 1

WHILE I WAS GROWING UP, MY DAD'S JOB required a long commute to New York City. A long train ride home topped off his already tough workday. Dad's impending arrival home was always full of anticipation for my sisters and brother and me. While Mom was cooking dinner, preparations were made for our nightly "surprise Dad" ritual. Seven o'clock would roll around, a car door would slam, another door would squeak open, and we would spring into action. Christine and Doug would sail over the couch and hunker down behind it, while I would head for the coat closet. Inevitably Paulette would freeze, yelling "Where should I hide?!" until I grabbed her and hunched back beneath the coats. Soon a booming voice would yell, "Where is everybody?" Unable to contain ourselves, we would all rush from our hiding places squealing "DAD!" and converge on him while he was still holding his briefcase.

His face never gave away the game. After the excitement died down, we would gather around the dinner table and talk to Dad. We told him our hopes and dreams, our daily triumphs and tragedies. He loved us, cared for us, and cherished us. He was (and is to this day) always happy, always loving, always kind. And always "surprised."

Inspired by my own father, it is my hope that *My Dad, My Hero* will make Dads everywhere laugh, reflect, and above all, realize how much they are appreciated.

—*Heather Russell-Revesz*

A Dad Is...

A father is a man who expects his children to be as good as he meant to be.

—CAROLYN COATS, author

To her the name of the father was another name for love.

—FANNY FERN, author

Fathers represent another way of looking at life—the possibility of an alternative dialogue.

—LOUISE J. KAPLAN, psychologist

Fathers, like mothers, are not born. Men grow into fathers and fathering is a very important stage in their development.

—David M. Gottesman

It doesn't matter who my father was; it matters who I remember he was.

—Anne Sexton

One father is more than a hundred schoolmasters.

—Seventeenth-century English proverb

Your father was ever virtuous, and holy men at their death have good inspirations.

—William Shakespeare, *The Merchant of Venice*

If there was ever a man
Who was generous, gracious, and good
That was my dad.

—"Song for My Father," written by Horace Silver

You know, fathers just have a way of putting everything together.

—Erika Cosby

I am your father. I brought you into this world, and I'll take you out!

—Bill Cosby as Cliff Huxtable, *The Cosby Show*

The thing to remember about fathers is, they're men. A girl has to keep it in mind: they are dragon-seekers, bent on improbable rescues. Scratch any father, you find someone chock-full of qualms and romantic terrors, believing change is a threat—like your first shoes with heels on, like your first bicycle it took such months to get.

—Phyllis McGinley, author

It is a wise father that knows his own child.

—William Shakespeare, *The Merchant of Venice*

All fathers are intimidating. They're intimidating because they are fathers. Once a man has children, for the rest of his life, his attitude is, "To hell with the world—I can make my own people. I'll eat whenever I want, I'll wear whatever I want, and I'll create whoever I want."

—Jerry Seinfeld

[A father] must be severe, firm, and stern when necessary, and he must always keep in mind the well-being, peace and tranquility of his entire family as the ultimate purpose of all his efforts and counsels for the guidance of the family in virtue and honor.

—LEON BATTISTA ALBERTI, architect

The father is always a Republican toward his son, and his mother's always a Democrat.

—ROBERT FROST

Fathers have a special excitement about them that babies find intriguing. At this time in his life an infant counts on his mother for rootedness and anchoring. He can count on his father to be just different enough from a mother. Fathers embody a delicious mixture of familiarity and novelty. They are novel without being strange or frightening.

—LOUISE J. KAPLAN, psychologist

It matters not that Time has shed His thawless
    snow upon your head,
For he maintains, with wondrous art,
Perpetual summer in your heart.

—WILLIAM HAMILTON HAYNE, "To My Father"

The kind of man who thinks that helping with the dishes is beneath him will also think that helping with the baby is beneath him, and then he certainly is not going to be a very successful father.

—ELEANOR ROOSEVELT

All the feeling which my father could not put into words was in his hand—any dog, child, or horse would recognize the kindness of it.

—FREYA STARK, author

my father moved through dooms of love
through sames of am through haves of give,
singing each morning out of each night
my father moved through depths of height

—E.E. CUMMINGS,
"my father moved through dooms of love"

A lifetime could not teach me what he knew!
I think he learned it in the school of love

—AGNES M. SLOANE, poet

How beautiful the world would be if all loved one
another as a father loves his own.

—JOHN GRAY

Each day of my life had been a gift from him.

—NELLIE PIKE RANDALL, poet

There is something ultimate in a father's love, something that cannot fail, something to be beloved against the whole world.

—FREDERICK FABER, priest

Be kind to thy father, for when thou wert young,
Who loved thee so fondly as he?
He caught the first accents that fell from thy tongue,
And joined in thy innocent glee.

—MARGARET COURTNEY, "Be Kind"

On Being a Dad

I do have a firm grasp of the fact that the most important job I'll ever do is that of parenting. It's that simple, folks. Kids are the sponge; you are the Supersoaker.

—DENNIS MILLER

By profession I am a soldier and take pride in that fact. But I am prouder—infinitely prouder—to be a father.

—GENERAL DOUGLAS MACARTHUR

Because, when you think about it, being a "daddy" is not just a name, it's a title. Like "duke" or "baron." And like any other self-respecting titles, it comes with certain privileges.

—PAUL REISER

Any parent wants the best for their children. I am not going to make a choice for my child on the basis of what is the politically correct thing to do.

—PRIME MINISTER TONY BLAIR

I love being a dad because no matter how much I smell, sweat, burp, or scratch, I still have someone who'll hug me.

—RAY ROMANO

After all, I'm your father. It's true if it hadn't been me it would have been someone else. But that's no excuse.

—Samuel Beckett

Until you have a son of your own...you will never know the joy, the love beyond feeling that resonates in the heart of a father as he looks upon his son. You will never know the sense of honor that makes a man want to be more than he is and to pass something good and hopeful into the hands of his son. And you will never know the heartbreak of the fathers who are haunted by the personal demons that keep them from being the men they want their sons to be.

—Kent Nerburn, theologian and author

The happiest days of my life have been the few which I have passed at home in the bosom of my family.

—Thomas Jefferson

What's the most special thing about being a father? Everything.

—Viggo Mortensen

It's a Tough Job

It is easier for a father to have children than for children to have a real father.

—POPE JOHN XXIII

The most difficult job in the world is not being president. It's being a parent.

—BILL CLINTON

The joys of parents are secret; and so are their griefs and fears.

—FRANCIS BACON

How can one say no to a child? How can one be anything but a slave to one's own flesh and blood?

—HENRY MILLER

What a dreadful thing it must be to have a dull father.

—MARY MAPES DODGE, author and editor

The fundamental defect of fathers is that they want their children to be a credit to them.

—BERTRAND RUSSELL

This is not to say that becoming a father automatically makes you a good father. Fatherhood, like marriage, is a constant struggle against your limitations and self-interests. But the urge to be a perfect father is there, because your child is a perfect gift.

—KENT NERBURN, theologian and author

If the new American father feels bewildered and even defeated, let him take comfort from the fact that whatever he does in any fathering situation has a 50 percent chance of being right.

—BILL COSBY

A man can only do what a man can do. But if he does that each day, he can sleep at night and do it again the next day.

—ALBERT SCHWEITZER

If you've never been hated by your child, you've never been a parent.

—BETTE DAVIS

You think it's easy being a lousy father?

—NICK TORTELLI, *Cheers*

A king, realizing his incompetence, can either delegate or abdicate his duties. A father can do neither. If only sons could see the paradox, they would understand the dilemma.

—MARLENE DIETRICH

Diogenes struck the father when the son swore.

—ROBERT BURTON

Fathers should be neither seen nor heard. That is the only proper basis for family life.

—OSCAR WILDE, *An Ideal Husband*

You've Got To Keep Your Sense of Humor

My father would have enjoyed what you have so generously said of me—and my mother would have believed it.

—Lyndon B. Johnson

Quitting is one of the few things I do well. I come from a long line of quitters. My father was a quitter, my grandfather was a quitter; I was raised to give up!

—George Costanza, *Seinfeld*

My father wove a tapestry of profanity which to this day is still hovering somewhere over Lake Michigan

—Ralphie, *A Christmas Story*

Simone Clouseau: Jacques would make a wonderful father. He has many redeeming qualities, you know.

Sir Charles: Name one.

Simone Clouseau: Oh, he's kind, loyal, faithful, obedient.

Sir Charles: You're either married to a boy scout or a dachshund.

—*The Pink Panther*

The American father...is never seen in London. He passes his life entirely in Wall Street and communicates with his family once a month by means of a telegram in cipher.

—Oscar Wilde

The place of the father in the modern suburban family is a very small one, particularly if he plays golf.

—BERTRAND RUSSELL

PRENTICE: You did have a father?
GERALDINE: Oh, I'm sure I did. My mother was frugal in her habits, but she'd never economize unwisely.

—JOE ORTON, *What the Butler Saw*

JUNE: That's a girl's name and her telephone number.
WARD: Well, what did you expect to find in a high school boy's clothes? A teething ring?

—WARD AND JUNE CLEAVER, *Leave it to Beaver*

The first half of our lives is ruined by our parents, and the second half by our children.

—CLARENCE DARROW

JIMMY: Say, Dave, is your mom still married to
    that guy? What's his name?
DAVE: My dad? Yes.

—NEWS RADIO

When I was a boy of fourteen, my father was so
ignorant I could hardly stand to have the old man
around. But when I got to be twenty-one, I was astonished at how much he had learned in seven years.

—MARK TWAIN

Humor is always based on a modicum of truth.
Have you ever heard a joke about a father-in-law?

—DICK CLARK

My father is probably the person that I got my
sense of humor from. I'm not saying I got his
sense of humor. I'm saying I got a sense of humor.

—RAY ROMANO

Raising Kids

Train up a child in the way he should go, and when he is old, he will not depart from it.

—PROVERBS 22:6

My father used to play with my brother and me in the yard. Mother would come out and say, "You're tearing up the grass."
"We're not raising grass," Dad would reply. "We're raising boys."

—HARMON KILLEBREW, baseball player

Boys and girls need chances to be around their father, to be enjoyed by him, and if possible to do things with him. Better to play fifteen minutes enjoyably and then say, "Now I'm going to read my paper" than to spend all day at the zoo crossly.

—Dr. Benjamin Spock

My father was frightened of his mother. I was frightened of my father and I am damned well going to see to it that my children are frightened of me.

—King George V

The father who does not teach his son his duties is equally guilty with the son who neglects them.

—Confucius

To be a successful father...there's one absolute rule: when you have a kid, don't look at it for the first two years.

—ERNEST HEMINGWAY

Parents decide to accept the responsibility of raising children. Any thanks they get for doing that is gravy. Grateful children are a blessing, but they aren't a necessity.

—DONALD C. MEDEIROS, psychologist

Raising human beings is a process of teaching children right from wrong and turning them into responsible individuals.

—NEIL KURSHAN, rabbi

Parenting forces us to get to know ourselves better than we ever might have imagined we could—and in many new ways.... We'll discover talents we never dreamed we had and fervently wish for others at moments we feel we desperately need them. As time goes on, we'll probably discover that we have more to give and can give more than we ever imagined. But we'll also find that there are limits to our giving, and that may be hard for us to accept.

—FRED ROGERS

As far as rearing children goes, the basic idea I try to keep in mind is that a child is a person. Just because they happen to be a little shorter than you doesn't mean they are dumber than you.

—FRANK ZAPPA

Govern a family as you would cook a small fish—very gently.

—CHINESE PROVERB

Parenting is a profoundly reciprocal process: we, the shapers of our children's lives, are also being shaped. As we struggle to be parents, we are forced to encounter ourselves; and if we are willing to look at what is happening between us and our children, we may learn how we came to be who we are.

—AUGUSTUS Y. NAPIER, family therapist

The average parent will go through the full gamut of ups and downs and trials and tribulations. The key is developing close ties with your children, teaching them to perform and function effectively.

—EARL WOODS, father of Tiger Woods

Fathers, provoke not your children to anger, lest they be discouraged.

—COLOSSIANS 3:20

A father is indeed miserable who holds the affection of his children only through the need they have of his assistance, if that may be called affection. He should make himself worthy of respect by his virtue and abilities, and worthy of love by his kindness and gentle manners.

—MICHEL DE MONTAIGNE, essayist

I am determined that my children shall be brought up in their father's religion, if they can find out what it is.

—CHARLES LAMB

Fathers and Sons

You hear it said that fathers want their sons to be what they feel they cannot themselves be, but I tell you it also works the other way. A boy wants something very special from his father.

—SHERWOOD ANDERSON

A wise son maketh a glad father.

—PROVERBS 10:1

Sons have always a rebellious wish to be disillusioned by that which charmed their fathers.

—Aldous Huxley

Leontine: An only son, sir, might expect more indulgence.

Croaker: An only father, sir, might expect more obedience.

—Oliver Goldsmith, *The Good-Natured Man*

Like father, like son.

—Fourteenth-century proverb

For thousands of years, father and son have stretched wistful hands across the canyon of time.

—Alan Valentine, author

We think our fathers fools, so wise we grow;
Our wiser sons, no doubt will think us so.

—ALEXANDER POPE

A man knows when he is growing old because he
begins to look like his father.

—GABRIEL GARCÍA MÁRQUEZ

One father is enough to govern one hundred
sons, but not a hundred sons one father.

—attributed to GEORGE HERBERT

No one would be foolish enough to choose war
over peace—in peace sons bury their fathers, but
in war fathers bury their sons.

—CROESUS OF LYDIA

The father in praising his son extols himself.

—CHINESE PROVERB

A man's desire for a son is usually nothing but the wish to duplicate himself in order that such a remarkable pattern may not be lost to the world.

—HELEN ROWLAND

For rarely are sons similar to their fathers: most are worse, and a few are better than their fathers.

—HOMER, *The Odyssey*

Fathers send their sons to college either because they went to college or because they didn't.

—L. L. HENDREN, educator

His little son into his bosom creeps,
The lively picture of his father's face.

—PHINEAS FLETCHER, poet

Perhaps host and guest is really the happiest relation for father and son.

—EVELYN WAUGH

If I'm more of an influence to your son as a rapper than you are as a father...you got to look at yourself as a parent.

—ICE CUBE

Dads and Daughters

There's something like a line of gold thread running through a man's words when he talks to his daughter, and gradually over the years it gets to be long enough for you to pick up in your hands and weave into a cloth that feels like love itself.

—JOHN GREGORY BROWN,
Decorations in a Ruined Cemetery

It is admirable for a man to take his son fishing, but there is a special place in heaven for the father who takes his daughter shopping.

—JOHN SINOR, author

People see Archie Bunker everywhere. Particularly girls—poor girls, rich girls, all kinds of girls are always coming up to me and telling me that Archie is just like their dad.

—CARROLL O'CONNOR

You're the end of the rainbow, my pot of gold,
You're daddy's little girl to have and hold.

—"DADDY'S LITTLE GIRL,"
written by Bobby Burke and Horace Gerlach

What I'd like my daughter to be is everything her mother is with some of my input.

—TIM ALLEN

Fathers can seem powerful and overwhelming to their daughters. Let her see your soft side. Express your feelings and reactions. Tell her where you came from and how you got there. Let her see that you have had fears, failures, anxious times, hurts, just like hers, even though you may look flawless to her.

—STELLA CHESS, psychiatrist, and
JANE WHITBREAD, author

I never wanted to marry anyone like my father; I always preferred those more shoddy.

—CHRISTINA STEAD, *Letty Fox*

'Cause my heart belongs to Daddy.

—COLE PORTER, "My Heart Belongs to Daddy"

When a father gives his daughter an emotional visa to strike out on her own, he is always with her. Such a daughter has her encouraging, understanding daddy in her head, cheering her on—not simply as a woman but as a whole, unique human being with unlimited possibilities.

—VICTORIA SECUNDA, psychologist

A father is always making his baby into a little woman. And when she is a woman he turns her back again.

—ENID BAGNOLD, author

She got her looks from her father. He's a plastic surgeon.

—GROUCHO MARX

I am dreaming, tonight, of an old southern town,
And the best friend that I ever had.
For I've grown so weary of roaming around,
And I'm going home to my dad.

—TANYA TUCKER, "Daddy and Home,"
written by Jimmy Rodgers

I could never dance around you, my father. No one ever danced around you. As soon as I left you, my father, the whole world swung into a symphony.

—ANAÏS NIN

Oh my God! I've become my father! I've been trying so hard not to become my mother, I didn't see this coming!

—RACHEL, *Friends*

She'll have fun, fun, fun,
till her daddy takes her T-Bird away

—THE BEACH BOYS, "Fun, Fun, Fun"

A Good Provider

If a man smiles at home somebody is sure to ask him for money.

—WILLIAM FEATHER, author

A father is a banker provided by nature.

—FRENCH PROVERB

HARVEY JR.: Say, Dad. Suppose you could lend me fifty for the trip home?
HARVEY: I hate these emotional farewells.

—BING CROSBY AND ANGUS DUCAN, in *High Time*

It doesn't make any difference how much money a father earns; his name is always Dad-Can-I.... Like all other children, my five have one great talent: they are gifted beggars. Not one of them ever ran into the room, looked up at me, and said, "I'm really happy that you're my father, and as a tangible token of my appreciation, here's a dollar."

—Bill Cosby

A truly rich man is one whose children run into his arms when his hands are empty.

—Traditional

Papa would do whatever he could
Preach a little gospel, sell a couple bottles of
    Doctor Good.

—Cher, "Gypsies, Tramps and Thieves,"
written by Bob Stone

All we have of freedom, all we use or know—
This our fathers bought for us long and long ago.

—RUDYARD KIPLING, The Old Issue

That is the thankless position of the father in the family—the provider for all, and the enemy of all.

—J. AUGUST STRINDBERG

Sometimes the poorest man leaves his children the richest inheritance.

—TRADITIONAL

Fame Game—
Famous Dads and Their Kids

Your daddy's upstairs. You can call him "Mr. President" now.

> —MAUDE SHAW to Caroline Kennedy on the morning after the 1960 presidential election

My father gave me a trumpet because he loved my mother so much.

> —MILES DAVIS

[Like] dealing with Dad—all give and no take.

—JOHN F. KENNEDY on negotiating with Soviet
Premier Nikita S. Khrushchev

I rarely disobeyed Daddy, both because of my respect for him and because I knew that punishment for my transgressions would be certain and sometimes severe.

—JIMMY CARTER

My dad's probably one of the kindest people in the world. When I was younger that's not how I was—I was a little spoiled brat.

—LEONARDO DICAPRIO

My father was a statesman; I'm a political woman. My father was a saint. I'm not.

—INDIRA GANDHI

I kept thinking what a wonderful old man he would have made if he had learned how…

—JACK HEMINGWAY on Ernest Hemingway

I don't mind looking into the mirror and seeing my father.

—MICHAEL DOUGLAS on Kirk Douglas

My father always wanted to be the corpse at every funeral, the bride at every wedding, and the baby at every christening.

—ALICE ROOSEVELT LONGWORTH on President Theodore Roosevelt

He's a good father.

—CARMELA SOPRANO, *The Sopranos*

My father is no different than any powerful man. Any man who's responsible for other people. Like a senator or a president.

—MICHAEL CORLEONE, *The Godfather*

When we worked together, you could see the pride in his eyes that his son had followed in his footsteps. On *Sea Hunt,* he was always like, "Those are my boys and they're actors like me."

—JEFF BRIDGES on Lloyd Bridges

My father was not a failure. After all, he was the father of a president of the United States.

—HARRY S. TRUMAN

Luke, I am your father.

—DARTH VADER, *Star Wars*

None of you can ever be proud enough of being the child of *such* a Father who has not his equal in this world—so great, so good, so faultless. Try, all of you, to follow in his footsteps and don't be discouraged, for to be really in everything like him, none of you, I am sure, will ever be. Try, therefore, to be like him in some points, and you will have acquired a great deal.

—Victoria, Queen of England

The Washington press corps thinks that Julie Nixon Eisenhower is the only member of the Nixon administration who has any credibility—and, as one journalist put it, this is not to say that anyone believes what she is saying but simply that people believe she believes what she is saying…it is almost as if she is the only woman in America over the age of twenty who still thinks her father is exactly what she thought he was when she was six.

—as reported by Nora Ephron

I'm sorry Mr. Davis. Sometimes my father says the wrong things.

—GLORIA, *All in the Family*

The Greatest Gift

Directly after God in heaven comes a papa.

—Wolfgang Amadeus Mozart

My father was my idol, so I always did everything like him.

—Earvin "Magic" Johnson

I could not point to any need in childhood as strong as that for a father's protection.

—Sigmund Freud

It's only when you grow up, and step back from him, or leave him for your own career and your own home—it's only then that you can measure his greatness and full appreciate it. Pride reinforces love.

—MARGARET TRUMAN

It no longer bothers me that I may be constantly searching for father figures; by this time, I have found several and dearly enjoyed knowing them all.

—ALICE WALKER

You have to dig deep to bury your daddy.

—GYPSY PROVERB

Whoever does not have a good father should procure one.

—FRIEDRICH NIETZSCHE

Men like my father cannot die. They are with me still, real in memory as they were in flesh, loving and beloved forever. How green was my valley then.

—IRVING PICHEL, *How Green Was My Valley*

The most important thing a father can do for his children is to love their mother.

—REVEREND THEODORE HESBURGH

Well, I wish you wouldn't because, aside from the fact that he has the same frailties as all human beings, he's the only father I have. Therefore, he is my model of manhood, and my estimation of him will govern the prospects of my adult relationships. So I hope you bear in mind that any knock at him is a knock at me, and I am far too young to defend myself against such onslaughts.

—LISA SIMPSON, *The Simpsons*

Fly on my father's wings
To places I have never been
There is so much I've never seen
And I can feel his heartbeat still
And I will do great things
On my father's wings

—THE CORRS, "On My Father's Wings"

Meet the
New Dad...

You know more than you think you do.

—Dr. Benjamin Spock

When Charles first saw our child Mary, he said all the proper things for a new father. He looked upon the poor little red thing and blurted, "She's more beautiful than the Brooklyn Bridge."

—Helen Hayes

A new father quickly learns that his child invariably comes to the bathroom at precisely the times when he's in there, as if he needed company. The only way for this father to be certain of bathroom privacy is to shave at the gas station.

—BILL COSBY

When Dad can't get the diaper on straight, we laugh at him as though he were trying to walk around in high-heel shoes. Do we ever assist him by pointing out that all you have to do is lay out the diaper like a baseball diamond, put the kid's butt on the pitcher's mound, bring home plate up, then fasten the tapes at first and third base?

—MICHAEL K. MEYERHOFF, educator

A baby has a way of making a man out of his father and a boy out of his grandfather.

—ANGIE PAPADAKIS

Men have their own questions, and they differ from those of mothers. New mothers are more interested in nutrition and vulnerability to illness while fathers tend to ask about when they can take their babies out of the house or how much sleep babies really need.

—KYLE D. PRUETT, child psychiatrist

My mother groaned! My father wept
Into the dangerous world I leapt:
Helpless, naked, piping loud,
Like a fiend hid in a cloud

—WILLIAM BLAKE, "Infant Sorrow"

A father who will pursue infant care tasks with ease and proficiency is simply a father who has never been led to believe he couldn't.

—MICHAEL K. MEYERHOFF, educator

...Same As
the Old Dad

We modern sensitive husbands realize that it's very
unfair to place the entire childcare burden on our
wives, so many of us are starting to assume maybe
3 percent of it. Even this is probably too much.

—DAVE BARRY

It is impossible to please all the world and one's
father.

—JEAN DE LA FONTAINE

My father hated radio and could not wait for television to be invented so he could hate that too.

—PETER DE VRIES, author

I just received the following wire from my generous daddy—"Dear Jack: Don't buy a single vote more than is necessary. I'll be damned if I'm going to pay for a landslide."

—JOHN F. KENNEDY

Papa was a rollin' stone,
Wherever he laid his hat was his home

—THE TEMPTATIONS, "Papa Was a Rollin' Stone," written by Barrett Strong

Jarrell was not so much a father…as an affectionate encyclopedia.

—MARY JARRELL

Santa looked like Daddy,
Or Daddy looked like him.
It's not the way I had him pictured,
Santa was a' much too thin.

> —PAUL BRANDT, "Santa Looked a Lot Like Daddy,"
> written by Buck Owens and Don Rich

Well let's face it, what right have you to a life, unless you devote it to dispelling the confines that our parents worked so hard to achieve... although don't forget we're all parents now.

> —DENNIS HOPPER

Your mama don't dance
And your daddy don't rock 'n roll

> —KENNY LOGGINS AND JIM MESSINA,
> "Your Mama Don't Dance"

My father never raised his hand to any one of his children, except in self-defense.

—FRED ALLEN

You know, he wanted to shoot the Royal Family, abolish marriage, and put everybody who'd been to public school in a chain gang. Yeah, he was an idealist, your dad was.

—*MORGAN: A SUITABLE CASE FOR TREATMENT*, written by David Mercer

What a Dad Wants

If there must be trouble let it be in my day, that my child may have peace.

—Thomas Paine

I have a dream…that my four little children will one day live in a nation where they will not be judged by the color of their skin but by the content of their character.

—Martin Luther King Jr.

Honour thy father and thy mother: that thy days
may be long upon the land which the Lord thy
God giveth thee.

—EXODUS 20:12

Okay, now look. My boss is going to be at this
picnic, so I want you to show your father some
love and or respect.

—HOMER SIMPSON, *The Simpsons*

The Child is father of the Man;
And I could wish my days to be
Bound each to each by natural piety.

—WILLIAM WORDSWORTH, "My Heart Leaps Up"

It is a wise child that knows his own father.

—HOMER

I happen temporarily to occupy this big White House. I am a living witness that any one of your children may look to come here as my father's child has. It is in order that each of you may have through this free government which we have enjoyed, an open field and a fair chance for your industry, enterprise, and intelligence; that you may all have equal privileges in the race of life, with all its desirable human aspirations.

—ABRAHAM LINCOLN

Let us now praise famous men, and our fathers that begat us.

—APOCRYPHA, Ecclesiasticus 44:1

My son, may you be happier than your father.

—SOPHOCLES

The best thing to give to your enemy is forgiveness; to an opponent, tolerance; to a friend, your heart; to your child, a good example; to a father, deference; to your mother, conduct that will make her proud of you; to yourself, respect; to all men, charity.

—Francis Maitland Balfour, embryologist

Dad had one great dream, a dream that had been handed down from generation to generation of male Bundys: to build their own room and live separately from their wives. Sadly, they all failed.

—Al Bundy, *Married with Children*

Father of fathers, make me one,
A fit example for a son.

—Douglas Malloch, inspirational poet

When a child, my dreams rode on your wishes,
I was your son, high on your horse,
My mind a top whipped by the lashes
Of your rhetoric, windy of course.

—SIR STEPHEN SPENDER

Let my experience supply your want of it, and
clear your way, in the progress of your youth,
of those thorns and briars which scratched and
disfigured me in the course of mine.

—LORD CHESTERFIELD to his son

Fatherly Advice

This above all: to thine own self be true.

—POLONIUS, from William Shakespeare's *Hamlet*

My prescription for success is based on something my father always used to tell me: you should never try to be better than someone else, but you should never cease trying to be the best you can be.

—JOHN WOODEN

Take example by your father, my boy, and be wery careful o' widders all your life, 'specially if they've kept a public-house, Sammy.

—MR. WELLER, from Charles Dickens'
The Pickwick Papers

When I was a small boy, my father told me never to recommend a church or a woman to anyone. And I have found it wise never to recommend a restaurant either. Something always goes wrong with the cheese soufflé.

—EDMUND G. LOVE, author

I was brought up in my father's house to believe in democracy. "Trust the people"—that was his message.

—WINSTON CHURCHILL

My father used to say, "Let them see you and not the suit. That should be secondary."

—CARY GRANT

I have found that the best way to give advice to your children is to find out what they want and then advise them to do it.

—HARRY S. TRUMAN

How true Daddy's words were when he said: "All children must look after their own upbringing." Parents can only give good advice or put them on the right paths, but the final forming of a person's character lies in their own hands.

—ANNE FRANK

But take your time, think a lot,
Why, think of everything you've got.
For you will still be here tomorrow, but your
dreams may not.

—CAT STEVENS, "Father and Son"

Father taught us that opportunity and responsibility go hand in hand.

—LAURENCE ROCKEFELLER

I once complained to my father that I didn't seem to be able to do things the same way other people did. Dad's advice? "Margo, don't be a sheep. People hate sheep. They eat sheep."

—MARGO KAUFMAN

JUNE: Now, why would a boy in high school
    possibly want to grow a mustache?
WARD: Don't you know?
JUNE: No.
WARD: June, behind every mustache, there's a
    woman...uh, that didn't come out quite
    right, but you know what I mean.

—WARD AND JUNE CLEAVER, *Leave It to Beaver*

My father told me there's no difference between a
black snake and a white snake. They both bite.

—THURGOOD MARSHALL

For my father, who used to sit, hour after hour,
night after night, outside our house in Africa,
watching the stars. "Well," he would say, "if we
blow ourselves up, there's plenty more where we
came from!"

—DORIS LESSING

I've always followed my father's advice: he told me, first, to always keep my word and, second, to never insult anybody unintentionally. If I insult you, you can be goddamn sure I intend to. And, third, he told me not to go around looking for trouble.

—JOHN WAYNE

As Time Goes By

And you, my father, there on the sad height,
Curse, bless, me now with your fierce tears, I pray.
Do not go gentle into that good night.
Rage, rage against the dying of the light.

—DYLAN THOMAS,
"Do Not Go Gentle into That Good Night"

Old as she was, she still missed her daddy sometimes.

—GLORIA NAYLOR

The cat's in the cradle and the silver spoon
Little boy blue and the man in the moon
"When you comin' home Dad?"
"I don't know when,
But we'll get together then
You know we'll have a good time then."

> —HARRY CHAPIN, "Cat's in the Cradle,"
> written by Harry and Sandy Chapin

As my soul slides down to die.
How could I lose him?
What did I try?
Bit by bit, I've realized
That he was here with me;
I looked into my father's eyes.

> —ERIC CLAPTON, "My Father's Eyes"

I got a name, I got a name
And I carry it with me like my daddy did
But I'm living the dream that he can't hear.

—JIM CROCE, "I Got a Name,"
written by C. Fox and N. Gimbel

My father died many years ago,
And yet when something special happens to me,
I talk to him secretly not really knowing whether
    he hears,
But it makes me feel better to half believe it.

—NATASHA JOSEFOWITZ, author

Lessons Learned

My daddy taught me how to work and play a
    tune on the fiddle
He taught me how to love and how to give just
    a little.

    —JOHN DENVER, "Thank God I'm a Country Boy,"
               written by John Sommers

My father didn't tell me how to live; he lived, and
let me watch him do it.

    —CLARENCE BUDINGTON KELLAND, screenwriter

I just owe almost everything to my father [and] it's passionately interesting for me that the things that I learned in a small town, in a very modest home, are just the things that I believe have won the election.

—Margaret Thatcher

I watched a small man with thick calluses on both hands work fifteen and sixteen hours a day. I saw him once literally bleed from the bottoms of his feet, a man who came here uneducated, alone, unable to speak the language, who taught me all I needed to know about faith and hard work by the simple eloquence of his example.

—Mario Cuomo

I remember a very important lesson that my father gave me when I was twelve or thirteen. He said, "You know, today I welded a perfect seam and I signed my name to it." And I said, "But, Daddy, no one's going to see it!" And he said, "Yeah, but I know it's there." So when I was working in kitchens, I did good work.

—Toni Morrison

According to Father's lexicon people who started on a job and didn't stay at it for fifty years were "quitters." If you stayed twenty years and then shifted to more congenial work you were a "drifter."

—Richard Bissell, humorist

Everything I ever learned as a small boy came from my father. And I never found anything he ever told me to be wrong or worthless. The simple lessons he taught me are as sharp and clear in my mind, as if I had heard them only yesterday.

–*How Green Was My Valley,*
based on the novel by Richard Llewellyn

For my father...manliness was not discussable, but had it been, it would have included a good business suit, ambition, paying one's bills on time, enough knowledge of baseball to hand out like tips at the barbershop, a residual but never foolhardy degree of courage, and an unbreakable reserve.

–Edmund White, author

He who is taught to live upon little owes more to his father's wisdom than he who has a great deal left him does to his father's care.

–William Penn

Of all nature's gifts to the human race, what is sweeter to a man than his children?

—CICERO

It's like my father used to say: "When I was a child, I thought as a child and spoke as a child...and when I became a man, I took that child out back and had him shot."

—BILL, *News Radio*

Sherman made the terrible discovery that men make about their fathers sooner or later...that the man before him was not an aging father but a boy, a boy much like himself, a boy who grew up and had a child of his own and, as best he could, out of sense of duty and, perhaps love, adopted a role called Being a Father so that his child would have something mythical and infinitely important: a Protector, who would keep a lid on all the chaotic and catastrophic possibilities of life.

—TOM WOLFE, *The Bonfire of the Vanities*

We have seen that men are learning that work, productivity, and marriage may be very important parts of life, but they are not its whole cloth. The rest of the fabric is made of nurturing relationships, especially those with children—relationships which are intimate, trusting, humane, complex, and full of care.

—KYLE D. PRUETT, child psychiatrist

O dearest, dearest boy! my heart
For better lore would seldom yearn,
Could I but teach the hundredth part
Of what from thee I learn.

—WILLIAM WORDSWORTH, "Anecdote for Fathers"

By the time a man realizes that maybe his father was right, he usually has a son who thinks he's wrong.

—CHARLES WADSWORTH

I have learned that my kids, like most kids, would rather work all night long in a salt mine than rake leaves at home.

—PHIL DONAHUE

So often, as the septuagenarian reflects on life's rewards, we hear that, "in the final analysis" of money, power, prestige, and marriage, fathering alone was what "mattered."

—KYLE D. PRUETT, child psychiatrist

Fathers' Legacies

What a father says to his children is not heard by the world, but it will be heard for posterity.

—JEAN PAUL RICHTER, novelist

His heritage to his children wasn't words or possessions, but an unspoken treasure, the treasure of his example as a man and a father.

—WILL ROGERS JR., actor

Commonly men will only be brave as their fathers
were brave, or timid.

—HENRY DAVID THOREAU

If you think about it seriously, all the questions
about the soul and the immortality of the soul
and paradise and hell are at bottom only a way
of seeing this very simple fact: that every action
of ours is passed on to others according to its
value, of good or evil, it passes from father to son,
from one generation to the next, in a perpetual
movement.

—attributed to ANTONIO GRAMSCI, political theorist

It is morning, Senlin says, and in the morning
When the light drips through the shutters like
    the dew,
I arise, I face the sunrise,
And do the things my fathers learned to do.

—CONRAD AIKEN, "Morning Song from 'Senlin' "

Many people now believe that if fathers are more involved in raising children than they were, children and sons in particular will learn that men can be warm and supportive of others as well as be high achievers. Thus, fathers' involvement may be beneficial not because it will help support traditional male roles, but because it will help break them down.

—JOSEPH H. PLECK, psychologist

You end up as you deserve. In old age you must put up with the face, the friends, the health, and the children you have earned.

—FAY WELDON

The father loves the son, and the son loves his sons.

—THE TALMUD

No child can be understood without knowing the parent.

—Orson Scott Card

When a man's father is alive, look at the bent of his will. When his father is dead, look at his conduct. If for three years he does not change from the way of the father, he may be called filial.

—Confucius

The sons of Pullman porters
And the sons of engineers
Ride their fathers' magic carpet made of steel.

—Arlo Guthrie, "The City of New Orleans," written by Steve Goodman

My father's father, his father's father, his—
Shadows like winds
Go back to a parent before thought, before speech,
At the head of the past.

—WALLACE STEVENS, "The Irish Cliffs of Moher"

A tree cannot stand without its roots.

—ZAIRIAN PROVERB

To be father of a nation is a great honor, but to be
the father of a family is a greater joy.

—NELSON MANDELA